© 2005 by
YouthLight, Inc.
Chapin, SC 29036
www.Youthlight.com

All rights reserved.

Written by Linda Swain Gill

Illustrated by David Lee Bass

Layout by Melinda Moseley

ISBN
1-889636-97-5

Library of Congress Number
2005921222

10 9 8 7 6 5 4 3 2 1
Printed in the United States

Dedication

This book is dedicated in loving memory of my father, Irving Thomas Swain who always believed in me, and to my son David Lee Bass, without whom the story never would have been told or creatively imagined on paper. And most importantly, it is dedicated to God, the dream-giver.

Important Information to Remember about Children and Grief

Children have sometimes been called "forgotten grievers." Adults often believe that children need to be protected from the reality of death because they are "too young to understand what is going on" and because the sadness and tears of others will "upset" them. Sometimes families, in an effort to "protect" them actually "neglect" them by not allowing them to do the things that often help most.

The truth is that children often become more upset, even very angry, if they are not included in family grief rituals. They should always be given a choice to be or not be with the family at the visitation or wake, and the funeral or memorial service. If children want to be included in the viewing of the body, it is not damaging to them unless there is no one available to explain things to them.

Things that can be damaging to them include:
- not being allowed to be with those they love and trust during a time that families need each other most;
- not being allowed to do something they want or need to do (e.g., saying goodbye, crying, taking a "play break", seeing or touching the person who died); or
- being forced to see or do something they do not want or need to do (e.g., touching the person who died or kissing them goodbye; being exposed to long periods of emotional intensity without a "play break").

It may be helpful to ask another trusted friend or family member to be with the child during the visitation, wake, funeral, or memorial service. That way, there is someone to explain things, answer questions, or take the child outside if he/she gets restless or needs a break from the emotional intensity of these times.

From the Author's Heart

This is a true story, told for the first time to my son David after my father died in February of 1985. David turned three the next month. Because he was so young, I doubted he would be able to understand much about what had happened. However, the evening of my father's funeral, he astounded me by asking, "Mommy, what's 'died'?" I decided, since he had asked the question, he deserved an answer understandable to a small child. This story was the answer I gave him. It was inspired by my love of analogies and teaching lessons through nature, and also by David's love of game-playing and bedtime stories.

One evening when David was ten years old, he asked if I remembered his Grandpa. He said he could remember sitting on my father's bed talking with him while he was ill. David also asked me if I remembered his Grandpa's death and the story I had told him. When he told me significant parts of the story, and clearly was not distressed by memories of that time in his life, I realized just how important the story had been for him, and I believed other children could benefit from hearing it also.

As a nurse specializing in crisis and grief, I began using the story with children who had experienced losses. Children and parents alike received the story enthusiastically and positively. Later, after I started practicing as a grief counselor, I knew the time had come to write the story for young children. I also knew that my son David, with his humor and artistic ability, was the only person who could ever capture the feelings and wonder of the story in pictures as I envisioned it. After all, it was his story! This book has been a labor of love for both of us, and I think my father would be pleased with the outcome.

My hope is that the story of Little Dave and his Grandpa will make it easier for parents and anyone who loves and cares about children to talk with them reassuringly and factually about death, dying, and the universal experience of grief.

"Mommy, What's 'Died'?"
The Butterfly Story

Written by Linda Swain Gill

Illustrated by David Lee Bass

The telephone rang. Mommy answered it and said, "Hello." It was Grandma. She had called to tell Mommy some sad news about Grandpa. When Mommy got off the phone she told Little Dave, "I have to go to see Grandma."

Mommy explained, "You know that Grandpa has been very sick a very long time. Most of the time when people get sick, they get well. But sometimes people have a sickness that doesn't get well, even when doctors and nurses try their best to make them get better. Grandpa's sickness is like that. Grandma needs me to come to be with her because Grandpa is probably going to die soon. You and Daddy will come to Grandma's house in a day or two to be with us."

Discussion
QUESTIONS:

1. Why is Mommy going to see Grandma?

2. How long had Grandpa been sick?

3. What did Mommy say usually happens when people get sick?

Little Dave was very quiet. Grandpa had been sick for as long as he could remember. He wondered about what Mommy had said about Grandpa dying, but he didn't ask any questions.

Discussion
QUESTIONS:

1. What do you think Little Dave was wondering about?

2. How do you think he felt? (worried, afraid, insecure, confused?)

3. Has anyone in your family ever died?

Daddy came home from work early to stay with Little Dave, and Mommy left to go to Grandma's house. The next day, Daddy and Little Dave went to Grandma's house too. Pastor Wilson was there from Grandma and Grandpa's church. Little Dave knew him very well and got a big hug from him. Pastor Wilson said, "I'm sorry that your Grandpa died, David. We will all miss him very much." Little Dave wondered where Grandpa had gone, but he didn't ask any questions.

Discussion
QUESTIONS:

1. What did Pastor Wilson say to Little Dave?

2. Why do you think everyone will miss Grandpa?

3. What was Little Dave wondering about?

The next day, Mommy said that soon it would be time to go to the funeral home for Grandpa's funeral. She explained that a funeral is an important time for people who loved Grandpa to remember special things about him. She said many people would be there to remember Grandpa and say "goodbye" to him. Little Dave didn't want to go. He didn't like to sit still for long. So he stayed at Grandma's house with some nice ladies while everybody else went to the funeral. Little Dave wondered about funerals and where Grandpa was, but he didn't ask any questions.

Discussion
QUESTIONS:

1. What do you think a funeral is?

2. Why didn't Little Dave want to go to the funeral?

3. What was Little Dave wondering about?

Later many people came back to Grandma's house. It was like a big party! People brought lots of food and stayed to visit and eat with Grandma, Mommy, Daddy, and Little Dave.

Discussion
QUESTIONS:

1. Why do you think there was a party at Grandma's house?

2. Why did people come to visit and bring food?

3. Why were some people laughing, and why were some crying?
(Note: emotional extremes are often seen after someone dies; these extremes are often very confusing to children)

People talked a lot about Grandpa. Some people were crying, and some of them were laughing. Little Dave wondered about the party, and why people were laughing and crying, but he didn't ask any questions.

Finally it was bedtime. Mommy put Little Dave in his bed upstairs at Grandma's house. He had slept there lots of times before. But this time he just couldn't go to sleep. He wondered about Grandpa. Where was he? He wondered about funerals and saying "goodbye" to Grandpa. He wondered about the party with the laughing and crying. Finally he needed to ask a question! "Momm-eee!" he called. Mommy came upstairs and said, "What's the matter, honey, can't you sleep?" Little Dave looked up at her and said solemnly, "Mommy, what's 'died'?"

Discussion
QUESTIONS:

1. Why couldn't Little Dave go to sleep?

2. What was he wondering about?

3. What do you think "died" means?

Note: As you read the story, play this game with your child.

Mommy thought a little while. Then she said, "I know! Let's play the 'Do-What-I Do' game!"

"Stick out your tongue like this…" She stuck out her tongue, and Little Dave did too.

"David, blink your eyes like this…" she said. She blinked her eyes, and Little Dave did too.

Then she said. "Stick your thumbs in your ears like this, and waggle your hands." She waggled her hands, and so did Little Dave.

"Now take a big deep breath like this…" she said. So Little Dave took a big deep breath and blew it out! Now…put your hands over your chest like this…can you feel your heart beating?" She put her hands over her chest, and Little Dave put his hands over his chest. He could feel his heart going bump-bump inside his chest. Little Dave wanted to feel Mommy's heart beating too.

Then Mommy said, "David, when we die, our body stops working, and we can't do any of those things any more. We can't stick out our tongue. Our eyes don't blink. And we can't waggle our hands. We can't take big deep breaths. Our lungs don't breathe. Our heart stops beating. We can't walk, or eat, or go to the bathroom, or go to sleep. After we die, we don't need to do any of that anymore because our body doesn't work. It just stops working!"

Discussion
QUESTIONS:

1. After someone dies, what stops working?
(The person's body stops working)

2. After someone dies, can the person stick out his tongue
or blink her eyes? Why not? (Because the person's body
doesn't work anymore)

3. After someone dies, why can't that person walk, eat, sleep,
or go to the bath room anymore? (Because the person's body
doesn't work anymore)

Next Mommy asked, "Do you remember the story we saw on TV the other day about the caterpillar and the butterfly?"

"Yes!" exclaimed Little Dave.

"Tell me about the caterpillar," said Mommy.

"He was fuzzy!" giggled Little Dave.

"Yes he was. He was crawling on a leafy branch. What did the caterpillar do next? Do you remember?" asked Mommy.

Discussion
QUESTIONS:

1. Have you ever seen a caterpillar?

2. What did it look like?

3. Did you touch it? What did it feel like?

"He made a cocoon!" said Little Dave, "And he was in it!"
"Yes," said Mommy, "He spun his cocoon all around himself and lived inside it for a while. And then what happened?"

Discussion
QUESTIONS:

1. What is a cocoon?

2. Do you know another name for a cocoon? (note: the technical name for a butterfly's cocoon is a chrysalis)

3. What do you think will happen next?

"He unzipped it!" exclaimed Little Dave happily.

"He sure did. And then what did he do?" asked Mommy.

"He came out!" said Little Dave.

"That's right. He came out of his cocoon. Did he still look like the same fuzzy caterpillar?" asked Mommy.

Discussion
QUESTIONS:

1. What is a funny thing about this cocoon?

2. Do you think cocoons really have zippers?

3. What do you think the caterpillar will look like when he comes out?

"No, Mommy. He was a butterfly!" giggled Little Dave.
"That's right," said Mommy. "He came out of the cocoon,
and he wasn't a caterpillar anymore. He dried his wings,
and then what did he do?"
"He flew away. He was a real butterfly!" said David in
amazement.

Discussion
QUESTIONS:

1. What happened to the caterpillar? (It changed into a butterfly)

2. What happened to his cocoon? (It got left behind when the butterfly moved out of it)

3. What happened to the butterfly? (It left the cocoon behind)

"That's right, David. He was a butterfly, and he flew away. I think that dying is a lot like that," said Mommy. "Grandpa lived in his body for a long, long time, just like the caterpillar lived in his cocoon. Grandpa's body was very old, and it wasn't working right anymore. So after a while Grandpa couldn't live in his old body anymore. It was time for him to die. His body stopped working, and he died. And just like the butterfly left his cocoon behind when he didn't need it anymore, Grandpa left his body behind. He didn't need it since it didn't work anymore."

Discussion
QUESTIONS:

1. Why did Grandpa die? (His body was very old, and it wasn't working right anymore.)

2. Do you think Grandpa turned into a butterfly and flew away? (Note: If the child says, "Yes", it will be important to separate fantasy from reality. One example of a "teasing" way to address the reality is to laugh and say: "No-o-o! Grandpa was a person, not a caterpillar! He lived in his body, not a cocoon!")

3. How was Grandpa like the butterfly?

"People usually get well when they are sick. Even when people are in the hospital or have an operation, usually they get better and get well. Most people don't die until they are very old like Grandpa. People can die when they are not old, but I don't expect that you or I will die until we are old."

Discussion
QUESTIONS:

1. What usually happens when people get sick, go to the hospital, or have an operation?

2. When do people usually die?
(Note: After a loss, some children fear that others they love will die too. The purpose of this question is to help children realize that this probably won't happen.)

3. Can people die when they are not old?
(Note: Some children may have begun to recognize that they will die someday. They may worry that they will die too. The purpose of this question is to reassure children that this probably won't happen.

Younger children will often express the desire to "go and see Grandpa." This is not a death wish. Young children simply do not realize the permanence of loss. Nor do they realize that the "place" that Grandpa has gone is not a physical place they can visit. They just want to "see Grandpa" again. As an illustration of their lack of being able to comprehend the permanence of death, young children have said things like, "My Grandpa is dead right now.")

Mommy continued, "We will miss Grandpa because, when people die, they don't live here with us anymore, and that makes us feel sad. Sometimes we may cry when we think about how much we miss Grandpa. If we need to cry, that is okay. Crying just means we miss him and wish we could see him again."

Discussion
QUESTIONS:

1. Why will Little Dave and his mother miss Grandpa?

2. Why do people cry sometimes after someone dies?

3. When Little Dave misses Grandpa how do you think he feels?
What do you think he does when he feels that way?

"So what happened to Grandpa? Where is he?" asked Little Dave. "Well," Mommy said, "Grandpa didn't need his body anymore. He left it behind just like the butterfly left his cocoon behind. The body is put into a special box called a casket. Then the casket is put into the ground in a special place called a grave. Since Grandpa didn't live in his body anymore, it was buried in a casket in the ground. Grandpa isn't cold, or hungry, or afraid of the dark because he doesn't live in his body anymore."

Discussion
QUESTIONS:

1. What happened to Grandpa? (He died and didn't need his body anymore)

(Note: If applicable, adapt the story here to include family beliefs about the concept of a "soul" or "spirit" that leaves the body behind.)

2. What is a casket? (Also can be called a coffin)

3. Why isn't Grandpa cold, or hungry, or afraid of the dark? (Because he isn't living in his body anymore.)

(Note: If the child's religious belief includes the concept of "soul sleep," you will need to adapt this part of the story accordingly)

Then Mommy asked, "Tomorrow would you like to go and see the place where Grandpa's body is buried?"

"Yes," said Little Dave.

"Well, tomorrow we will go there. It is a place called a cemetery. And we will find Grandpa's grave. There will be lots of flowers there. Later there will be a special stone with Grandpa's name on it to mark the place where his body got buried. There are many other graves there so that you can see what the stone will look like."

"And guess what? There is a little pond nearby with some ducks. Shall we take some bread to feed the ducks?" asked Mommy.

Discussion
QUESTIONS:

1. One of the ducks in the picture looks angry. Do you think Little Dave ever feels angry? How do you think he feels since his Grandpa died?

2. Why will a stone be placed on Grandpa's grave?

3. Is Grandpa under the ground?

(Note: If the child says, "Yes" but the family believes the soul has gone elsewhere, be sure to explain that only Grandpa's body, like the butterfly's cocoon, was buried. Then talk about family's beliefs about where Grandpa's soul is now.)

"Yes! I want to go see the grave and the ducks!" said Little
Dave. He yawned. "I'm sleepy," he said.
"Sweet dreams, " said Mommy. "We can talk about
Grandpa anytime we want to, and we will always keep spe-
cial memories of Grandpa alive in our hearts." Then she
kissed him goodnight.

Discussion
QUESTIONS:

1. Will Mommy and Little Dave forget all about Grandpa?

2. What things can they do to remember him?

3. What keeps people alive in our hearts?

That night Little Dave dreamed about the ducks and about Grandpa. It was a happy dream about feeding the ducks...

...and about Grandpa picking
him up high in the air!

About the Author

Linda Gill has Master's degrees in both Counseling and Parent-Infant Nursing. She is in private practice as a counselor providing services for clients who have experienced any kind of life loss. She has an extensive clinical nursing background including maternity nursing as well as intensive care nursing for adults, children, and infants. She worked in a hospital setting from 1991-1996 as a Clinical Nurse Specialist providing crisis and bereavement intervention for families who experienced miscarriage, stillbirth, or the critical illness or death of an infant or child. In 1995, she co-founded the SIDS Coalition in South Carolina, later assuming the position of Executive Director for the South Carolina SIDS Alliance affiliate. In addition to her earned degrees, she is also a Resolve Through Sharing® (RTS) Coordinator through Bereavement Services®, La Crosse, Wisconsin. She is available to speak, provide classes, or provide consulting services related to grief and loss.

About "Joy in the Mourning"®

"Joy in the Mourning"®

"Joy in the Mourning"® was founded by Linda Gill in 1996. The purpose of "Joy in the Mourning"® is to provide grief counseling and support services to assist individuals and families toward healing through the process of mourning their losses. Losses are a part of life. The aftermath of a significant loss, particularly a death, can affect personal relationships, sometimes disrupting them in unhealthy or painful ways. Marriages and parent-child relationships can suffer. Friendships can be affected. Even an individual's professional life can be affected because of the mental and emotional exhaustion associated with normal grief.

The service mark, "Joy in the Mourning"® was inspired by an ancient psalm which has been adapted to assert that "weeping may endure through the long night of sorrow, but joy will return in the mourning." The goal of "Joy in the Mourning"® is to help people mourn in healthy ways that bring them back to joy in life.

The sun and clouds logo graphically represents the process of recovery from grief. The sun is partially obscured by silver-lined clouds with golden rays of light breaking through them. The clouds obscuring the sun represent the sadness of grief shrouding the joy of life. The silver outlines of the clouds represent hope for the future. The rays breaking through the clouds represent the way in which healthy mourning allows those who have experienced a loss to experience joy once again.

Please visit our website: joyinthemourning.com